Countries Around the World

England

Claire Throp

www.raintreepublishers.co.uk
Visit our website to find out more information about Raintree books.

To order:

☎ Phone 0845 6044371

🖷 Fax +44 (0) 1865 312263

✉ Email myorders@raintreepublishers.co.uk

Customers from outside the UK please telephone +44 1865 312262

Raintree is an imprint of **Capstone Global Library Limited**, a company incorporated in England and Wales having its registered office at 7 Pilgrim Street, London, EC4V 6LB – Registered company number: 6695582

Text © Capstone Global Library Limited 2012
First published in hardback in 2012
The moral rights of the proprietor have been asserted.

Edited by Louise Galpine, Kate DeVilliers, and Laura Knowles
Designed by Richard Parker
Original illustrations © Capstone Global Library Ltd 2011
Illustrated by Oxford Designers & Illustrators
Picture research by Liz Alexander
Originated by Capstone Global Library Ltd
Printed in China by CTPS

ISBN 978 1 406 22799 4 (hardback)
15 14 13 12 11
10 9 8 7 6 5 4 3 2 1

British Library Cataloguing in Publication Data
Throp, Claire.
England. -- (Countries around the world)
942'.086-dc22
A full catalogue record for this book is available from the British Library.

Acknowledgments
We would like to thank the following for permission to reproduce photographs: Alamy pp. **6** (© Mary Evans Picture Library), **11** (© North Wind Picture Archives), **32** (© Chris Wood), **35** (© Richard Peel); Corbis pp. **8** (© Nik Wheeler), **12** (© Hulton-Deutsch Collection), **24** (© David Leahy/cultura), **33** (© Toby Melville/Reuters); Getty Images pp. **21** (Daniel Berehulak), **30** (AFP), **39** (Dorling Kindersley); iStockphoto p. **37** (© Martin Lovatt); Photolibrary p. **27** (Monkey Business Images Ltd); Shutterstock pp. **5** (© Steve Smith), **7** (© Dmitry Chernobrov), **15** (© Richard Bowden), **16** (© Joop Snijder jr), **19** (© Paul Gibbings), **18** (© Rafal Olkis), **23** (© r.nagy), **25** (© Lara65), **28** (© Edyta Pawlowska), **29** (© Monkey Business Images), **31** (© Andry Alamsyah), **46** (© Gary Blakeley).

Cover photograph of two deck chairs on the beach at Brighton, with the Palace Pier in the background reproduced with permission of Alamy/© M J Perris.

We would like to thank Rob Bowden for his invaluable help in the preparation of this book.

Every effort has been made to contact copyright holders of material reproduced in this book. Any omissions will be rectified in subsequent printings if notice is given to the publisher.

Disclaimer
All the Internet addresses (URLs) given in this book were valid at the time of going to press. However, due to the dynamic nature of the Internet, some addresses may have changed, or sites may have changed or ceased to exist since publication. While the author and publisher regret any inconvenience this may cause readers, no responsibility for any such changes can be accepted by either the author or the publisher.

Contents

Some words are printed in bold, **like this**. You can find out what they mean by looking in the glossary.

Introducing England

What comes to mind when you think about England? Historic buildings? Green fields? Fish and chips? Cricket? Wimbledon? England is known for all these things and more.

England or Britain?

There is often confusion about the difference between England, Great Britain, and the United Kingdom (UK). England is part of an island that includes Scotland and Wales as well as many smaller islands around the coast. These countries make up Great Britain. The UK includes Northern Ireland, too.

Invasion by many forces over the years has led to a mixture of **cultures** and characteristics. This has particularly affected the English language, although most common words come from the Anglo-Saxon period.

My word!

Where do English words come from?

street	*straet*	(Romans)
rose	*rosa*	(Romans)
passport	*passeport*	(French)
landscape	*landschap*	(Dutch)

Saint George

Saint George is England's patron saint and his feast day is celebrated on 23 April. King Edward III made him a saint in the mid-14th century. Saint George is famous for slaying a dragon, but this is probably just a story. All we do know is that he was a Christian soldier, killed in the early 4th century. It is also thought that he never actually set foot in England!

Small but attractive

England is a small country but it attracts millions of visitors every year. People come to see unspoilt countryside, and experience culture in the form of art, theatre, and music. England's great history also draws people to the country.

Many people visit North Yorkshire to go walking and take in the beautiful scenery.

History: invasion and empire

There is evidence that people lived in England 700,000 years ago. Stone tools have been found in Suffolk. England was later invaded by people from central Europe – the Celts – and by about 500 BC around 20 **tribes** lived in England.

The Romans

The Romans successfully invaded England in AD 43 under Emperor Claudius. They were soon in control of an area that included most of England and Wales, which they called Britannia. The Romans were responsible for bringing stability and wealth to England. In AD 313 they introduced **Christianity**. The Romans also left England with baths and a system of roads, among other things. They left around AD 410.

BOUDICCA

Boudicca was the queen of the Iceni, a tribe that lived in the area around Norfolk and Suffolk. She is famous for very nearly defeating the Romans in England around AD 60. Boudicca and her army got as far as Londinium (London), and killed many Roman soldiers, but the Romans crushed them in the end.

Boudicca Queen of the Iceni.

Hadrian's Wall was built to separate England and Scotland and was created in Roman times. It is named after Emperor Hadrian.

Viking invasion

Another invasion followed in AD 865, this time by the Vikings. They came mainly from Denmark and conquered the east and northeast of England. Their capital city was Jorvik, which is now called York. They moved south and came up against Alfred, the king of Wessex. He is famous for pushing the Vikings back to the north. Alfred saved the English language by using it to **unite** the tribes he ruled over. He did this by using English to educate his people.

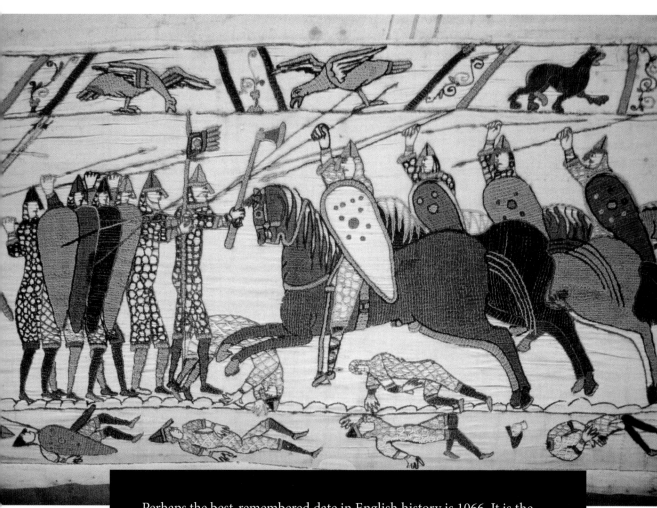

Perhaps the best-remembered date in English history is 1066. It is the date of the Battle of Hastings. William of Normandy (from France) fought King Harold for the crown of England, and won. The Bayeux Tapestry tells what happened during the Norman invasion.

A new church

Henry VIII is famous as the king who had six wives. While married to Catherine of Aragon, Henry fell in love with Anne Boleyn. Henry asked the **pope**, the leader of the Roman Catholic religion, to end his marriage with Catherine. The pope refused so Henry created a new church, the Church of England, with himself as the head. He was then able to end his own marriage.

QUEEN ELIZABETH I (1533-1603)

Elizabeth I, daughter of Henry VIII and Anne Boleyn, came to the throne when she was 25, and ruled for 45 years. During this time England became rich and powerful and the period is known as the Golden Age. Elizabeth famously never married and declared "I have already joined myself in marriage to a husband, namely the kingdom of England."

English Civil War (1642–49)

The Civil War was between the Royalists (or Cavaliers) and Oliver Cromwell's army, the Parliamentarians (or Roundheads). Many people thought King Charles I had too much power and Parliament wanted more for themselves. The Parliamentarians won the war and England became a **republic** under Cromwell's leadership. Cromwell's son took over after Oliver's death, but it was not long before Parliament asked Charles I's son to become King Charles II. However, Parliament now had far more control.

Great Britain

In 1536 the Act of Union joined England and Wales. In 1707 an Act of Union also joined Scotland to England and the three countries became Great Britain. They were ruled by one parliament, based in London.

Daily life

In 1665 the **Great Plague** killed nearly one-fifth of the population of London. The plague spread to other places, such as Eyam in the north of England. The village closed itself off so that the disease could not spread further. Food was left outside the village for the villagers inside to collect. They even had to dig their own graves.

American independence

The American War of Independence (1775–1783) was fought between Britain and America, a country that Britain ruled at the time. America no longer wanted to be under British control. America eventually won the war and Britain gave up its claims to the American states.

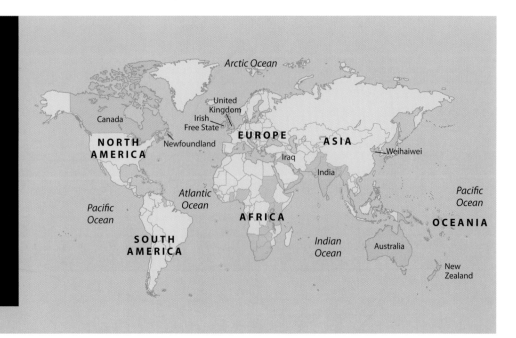

The British Empire was the largest empire the world had ever seen. At its height, it covered about a quarter of the world's land area, shown here in pink.

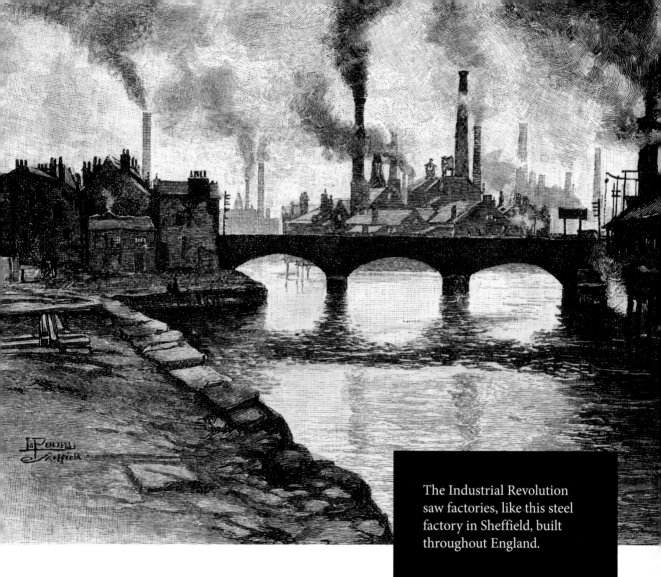

The Industrial Revolution saw factories, like this steel factory in Sheffield, built throughout England.

The Industrial Revolution

The **Industrial Revolution** was well under way when Queen Victoria came to the throne in 1837. New machines such as the spinning jenny for spinning cotton were invented that manufactured products quickly and in large numbers. Transport improved and trains carrying raw materials and goods ran the length of the country. England changed from a country mainly based on farming to one based on manufacturing.

Queen Victoria died in 1901. She had reigned longer than any other monarch. The expansion of the **British Empire** came to an end with her death.

Two World Wars

About one million Britons died in World War I (1914–1918), mainly while fighting in Belgium and France. However, in World War II (1939–1945) England was bombed by the Germans. London was badly affected. Thousands of children were evacuated (moved out) to live with families in rural areas. Prime Minister Winston Churchill became a national hero, inspiring the British to fight the Germans.

Daily life

During World War II, families had to survive on **rations** because the Germans prevented food ships from reaching Britain. People took ration books to shops and got a set amount of food in return for stamps. Potato Pete and Dr Carrot were cartoon characters that encouraged people to grow their own vegetables.

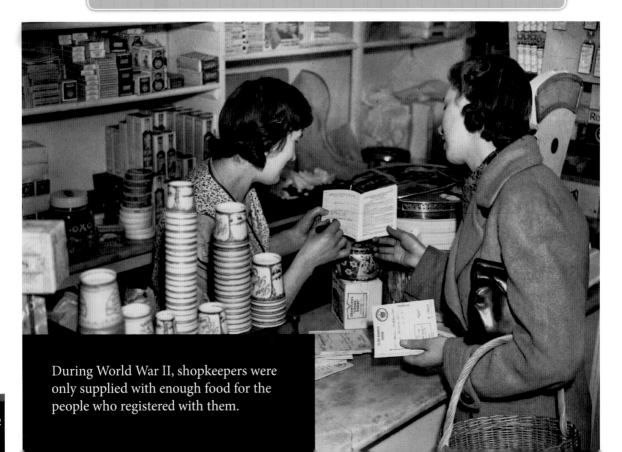

During World War II, shopkeepers were only supplied with enough food for the people who registered with them.

After the war

Britain's economy suffered after World War II. The country had borrowed money from the United States to help pay for the War, but then struggled to pay it back. Britain was in a weakened state and was unable to stop many countries within the British Empire from gaining independence by the 1960s. In 1973 the UK joined the European Economic Community, now known as the **European Union**.

Margaret Thatcher, the leader of the Conservative Party, became Britain's first woman prime minister in 1979. She led the country until 1990. In 1997, the Labour Party won the election and Tony Blair became Prime Minister.

21st century England

The global financial crisis that began in 2008 brought Britain into **recession**. The **economy** slowed, with people losing their jobs and unable to spend as much money as before. The general election of 2010 was very close. The Labour Party had been in power but a new government was formed, led by the Conservative party with Liberal Democrat party support.

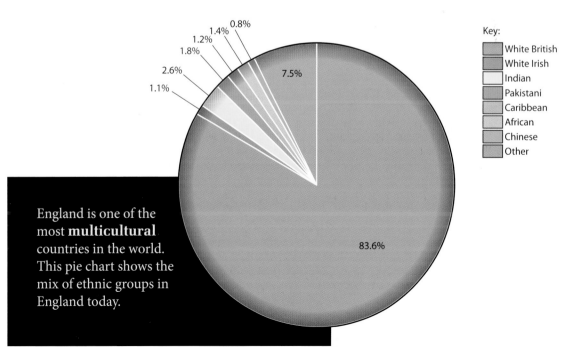

0.8%
1.4%
1.2%
1.8%
2.6%
1.1%
7.5%
83.6%

Key:
- White British
- White Irish
- Indian
- Pakistani
- Caribbean
- African
- Chinese
- Other

England is one of the most **multicultural** countries in the world. This pie chart shows the mix of ethnic groups in England today.

Regions and resources: a varied landscape

England is one of three countries on one island. Scotland is to the north of England and Wales to the west. Nowhere in England is far from the sea – the furthest is 125 kilometres (77 miles) from the coast. The seas that surround England are the North Sea, Irish Sea, and Atlantic Ocean. The English Channel is to the south and separates England from mainland Europe. At its narrowest point, France is just 34 kilometres (21 miles) away.

England is divided into nine regions and 45 counties. The number of counties has changed over the years. For example, Yorkshire, a traditional county, was split into four in 1974.

This map shows some of the key natural features of England.

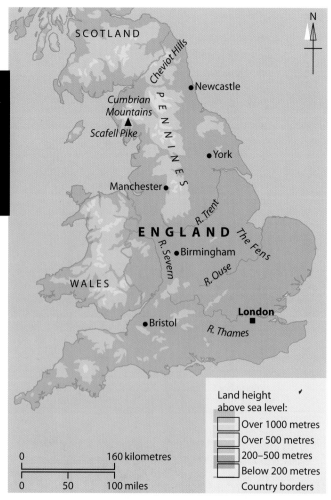

SCOTLAND

Cheviot Hills

● Newcastle

Cumbrian Mountains

P E N N I N E S

▲ Scafell Pike

● York

Manchester ●

R. Trent

E N G L A N D

The Fens

R. Severn

● Birmingham

R. Ouse

WALES

London ■

● Bristol

R. Thames

Land height above sea level:

- Over 1000 metres
- Over 500 metres
- 200–500 metres
- Below 200 metres
- Country borders

0   160 kilometres

0   50   100 miles

Climate

English people are well known for talking about the weather. This is because it is so changeable. One of the reasons for this is that England is part of an island. English summers are usually cooler than in Europe but winters are normally milder. It is overcast on more than half the days of the year.

Landscape

The landscape in England varies from rolling hills, waterfalls, rivers, and lakes to the flat marshlands of the Fens and the Cumbrian Mountains. However, there are no real extremes. For example, Scafell Pike in the Lake District is the highest mountain at only 978 metres (3,208 feet).

This bar chart shows the average rainfall and maximum and minimum temperatures in England throughout the year.

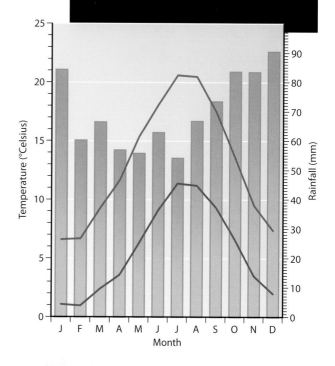

The Fens have been affected by climate change. It is thought that 400,000 hectares of land may be lost under water by 2030.

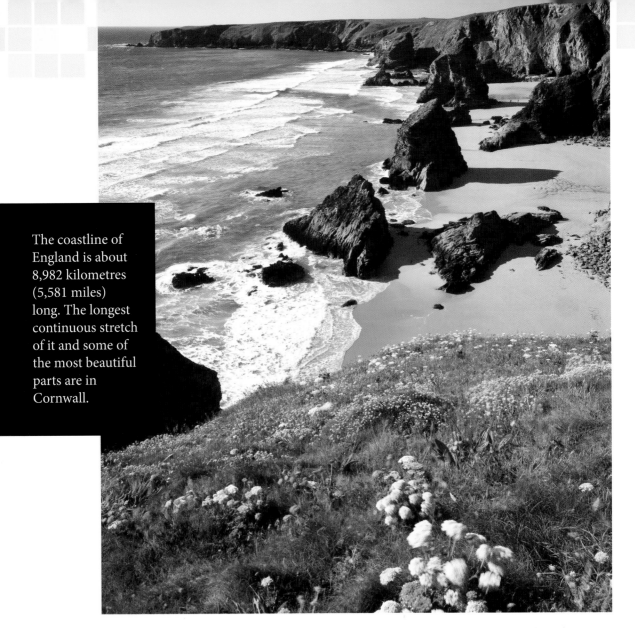

The coastline of England is about 8,982 kilometres (5,581 miles) long. The longest continuous stretch of it and some of the most beautiful parts are in Cornwall.

Rivers and mountains

The River Thames is the longest river in England at 338 kilometres (210 miles). It begins near Cirencester in the west and travels as far as the North Sea. The Pennines mountain range is often called "the backbone of England" as it runs down the middle of the country, separating the northeast and the northwest.

Resources and trade

Coal and salt are among England's main **resources**. Sand, gravel, and clay provide raw materials for the construction industry. UK **trade** is mainly with Europe and the United States.

Jobs

In England there has been a shift from traditional industries, such as farming, and heavy industry, such as shipbuilding, towards services, such as finance or restaurants. However, cattle and sheep are farmed for the meat and milk they provide, and farms produce wheat, barley, and vegetables. About one-fifth of English workers have manufacturing jobs, such as food processing, textiles, and cars. Finance is a big part of the English economy. London is a major world centre for banking and finance, but other cities, including Manchester, are also important. Tourism in England provides a lot of jobs in hotels and restaurants in tourist areas.

Economy

The 2008 global financial crisis affected the UK particularly badly. The economy slowed down. Unemployment rose to its highest since 1994. **Debt** became a huge problem that the new government set to work on reducing straight away. Government debt had reached very high levels.

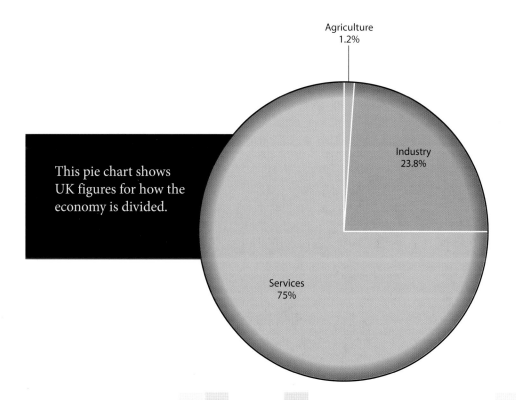

Agriculture
1.2%

Industry
23.8%

Services
75%

This pie chart shows UK figures for how the economy is divided.

Wildlife: natural England

While much of England's landscape has been changed by people, there are still many areas where nature thrives.

Birds

The Royal Society for the Protection of Birds (RSPB) works for the protection of birds and wildlife and has over a million members. It's the biggest **conservation** charity in Europe. Birds that are common in England include robins and blackbirds.

Animals

There are few **species** of amphibian or reptile in England. The adder, the only poisonous snake, is rare. Common animals include mammals, such as rabbits, grey squirrels, and foxes. **Endangered** animals include the water vole and the red squirrel.

It is thought that hedgehogs may be extinct in the UK by 2025. This is partly due to the loss of their natural **habitat**.

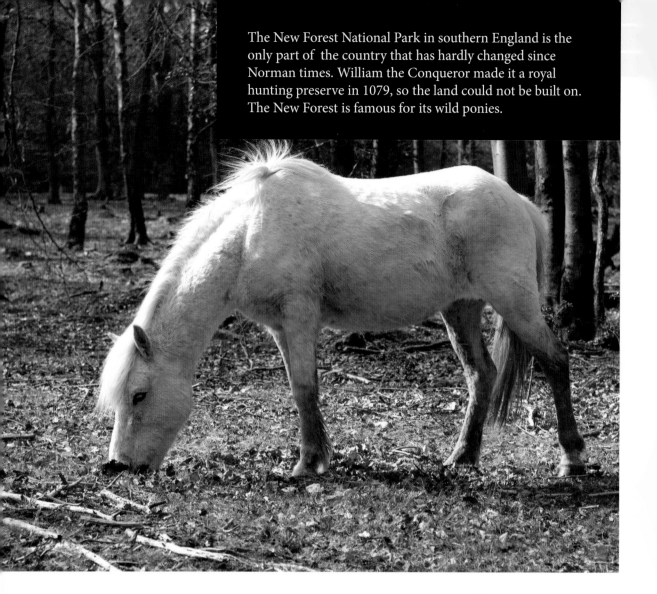

The New Forest National Park in southern England is the only part of the country that has hardly changed since Norman times. William the Conqueror made it a royal hunting preserve in 1079, so the land could not be built on. The New Forest is famous for its wild ponies.

National Parks

National Parks are areas protected for their natural beauty and wildlife. In England they are often privately owned but are free and open to the public. Unlike national parks in some other countries, which are wilderness areas, in England they often include roads and villages. There are ten National Parks in England including the Lake District in the north, which is famous for its lakes. Dartmoor has the largest open space in southern England, surrounded by rocky land and valleys. The Norfolk and Suffolk Broads are also usually included in the list of National Parks although they were created separately. These protected areas cover about eight per cent of England.

Reduced wildlife areas

England is a small country with a large population, so wildlife habitats are often under threat and sometimes destroyed. Destruction of **hedgerows** has meant that some birds, such as skylarks, have become rare in the countryside. Environmental pollution, such as chemicals used by farmers, and the introduction of species from other countries, has also affected England's wildlife.

As people have become more aware of habitat loss, campaigns have tried to stop habitat destruction. The National Forest in central England is one example. Nearly 8 million trees have been planted, helping to provide new habitats for wildlife. Farmers have also been offered financial help to reduce the amount of chemicals that end up in rivers, and to protect hedgerows and leave borders around fields to encourage wildlife back.

YOUNG PEOPLE

Eco-Schools is an international programme that helps schools to become more **eco-friendly**. School children run the programme themselves. They look at how environmentally-friendly their school is and then choose what they want to improve, such as litter, waste, or energy, and how they will do it. Awards are gained when a school successfully shows improvements.

Getting rid of waste

Much of England's rubbish is buried in **landfill sites**. Environmental campaigners think these sites may be full by 2015. Local governments are encouraging people to recycle as much as possible and a landfill **tax** is charged on every tonne of waste. One of the other options is incineration (burning), but there are environmental problems with this, too. Unless rubbish is burnt at a particular temperature, it can release dangerous poisons into the air.

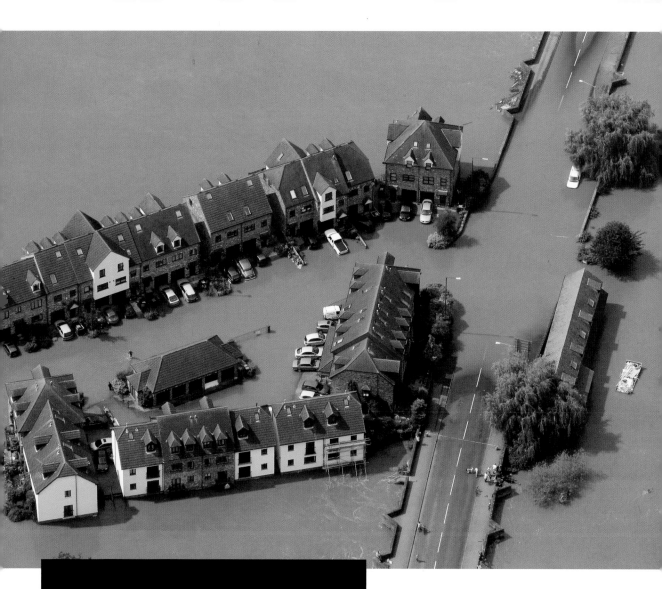

An increasingly common natural disaster to affect England is flooding. In recent years heavy rain has destroyed people's homes in places such as Tewkesbury.

Infrastructure: constitutional monarchy

The UK is a constitutional monarchy. The **monarch** is the **head of state** but has no real power. The prime minister is the head of government. Along with Parliament, he or she is responsible for the day-to-day running of the country.

Parliament is made up of two houses: the **House of Commons** and the **House of Lords**. Parliamentary elections are held at least every five years. Everyone over the age of 18 is allowed to **vote** for a Member of Parliament (MP). Local government includes county councils, which deal with education and planning. District councils deal with matters such as waste collection and housing.

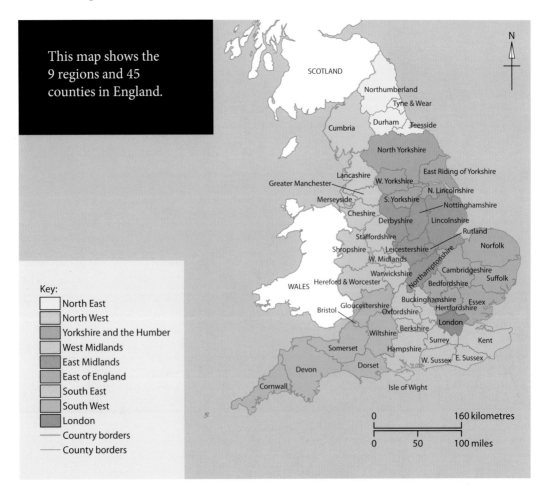

This map shows the 9 regions and 45 counties in England.

Key:
- North East
- North West
- Yorkshire and the Humber
- West Midlands
- East Midlands
- East of England
- South East
- South West
- London
- —— Country borders
- —— County borders

The Houses of Parliament are based at Westminster in London.

European Union and NATO

The UK has been a member of the European Union (EU) since 1973. However, the UK chose to keep pound sterling as the **currency** rather than changing to the euro, the EU's currency, as most other European countries did. The UK is also a member of NATO and the United Nations, which aims to bring peace to troubled areas of the world.

THE PANKHURSTS

Emmeline Pankhurst and her daughter Christabel led the fight to get British women the vote. At first Emmeline fought for women to be allowed to vote in local elections. Then, along with her daughters, she founded a group whose members became known as suffragettes. Their actions shocked Britain as they smashed windows, got arrested, and went on hunger strike. Women gained the vote in 1918, but only for those aged over 30. It was 1928 before women's voting rights were the same as men's.

Health care

The National Health Service (NHS) was set up in 1948. It allows everyone living in England, no matter how rich or poor, to see a doctor or get hospital care free of charge. There are sometimes long waits for major treatment so some people, if they can afford it, pay for private treatment.

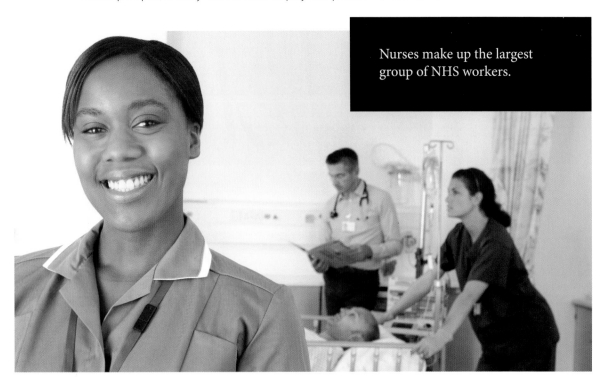

Nurses make up the largest group of NHS workers.

Media

The BBC is a public service broadcaster. This means that they must provide television and radio programmes that appeal to many different people. The money to finance the BBC comes from a licence fee paid by everyone who owns a television. Commercial television channels, such as ITV, have to aim for as many viewers as possible. Their money comes from companies wishing to advertise their products during programmes. More viewers mean more money from advertisers because their products will reach more people.

There are 10 national newspapers in England as well as many local ones. The national papers range from tabloids, which include lots of scandalous stories, to broadsheets, which are more serious.

Technology

In 2009, more than 18 million homes in the UK had access to the Internet. About 90 per cent of those had **broadband**. **Rural** areas have more difficulty getting Internet access and mobile phone signals.

YOUNG PEOPLE

In a recent poll, it was found that 79.1 per cent of children aged between 7 and 11 own their own mobile, but only 72.7 per cent own their own books. Many people worry that children's reading skills will only worsen as they spend more time on their phone. What do you think?

Many children in England spend a lot of time talking or texting on their mobile phone!

School life

School in England is free and children must go to school between the ages of five and sixteen. Many children also go to nursery school from the age of three. Some children go to fee-paying schools. All schools teach the same subjects as part of the **National Curriculum**. Subjects are taught to the same level in all schools.

The school year is usually divided into three terms, from the beginning of September until the end of July. This means that school holidays are at Christmas, Easter, and for six weeks during the summer.

YOUNG PEOPLE

School is from Monday to Friday only, unlike some countries where children have to go to school on Saturday. The school day usually lasts from around 9 a.m. until about 3.30 p.m. Most children stay in school for lunch, either buying a hot meal or bringing a packed lunch.

Primary school

In primary school children have lessons on literacy, numeracy, religious education, art, music, and PE. They also study simple science, history, and geography, as well as personal and social skills.

Secondary school

At the age of 11 children go to secondary school. Children study a range of subjects including at least one foreign language. At the age of 14 they begin to study for GCSEs. Depending on their GCSE exam results they can then go on to do A-levels or courses at college.

University

From the age of 18, young people can continue their education at university. This usually involves studying a subject in detail. England has some of the oldest universities in the world, including Oxford and Cambridge.

Culture: pubs, Proms, and cheese-rolling

England is not known for its great food but traditional English meals can be a real treat. They include the Sunday roast, fish and chips, and puddings such as apple pie. Tea and coffee are popular drinks. Most people in England buy their food from supermarkets. Butchers, grocers, and bakers are becoming less common as a result of this. Farmers' markets can still be found in some towns a couple of times a week.

Pubs

A typical English tradition is going to the pub for a pint of beer! Nowadays this may be accompanied by a live band or by sport – usually football – on a big screen. Many pubs have outdoor seating so that families can go for lunch together. Some pubs even have activities for children, such as a bouncy castle in the garden.

The London Eye opened in 2000 and has 3.5 million visitors a year. From the London Eye you can see up to 40 kilometres (25 miles) in all directions.

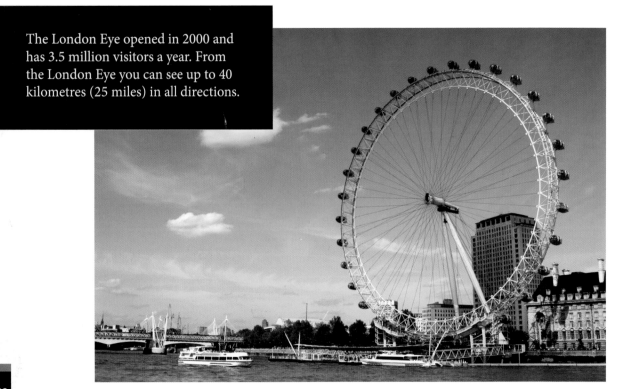

Apple crumble recipe

Ask an adult to help you make this delicious pudding.

Ingredients

- 450 grams apples
- 300 grams plain flour
- 200 grams butter
- 175 grams brown sugar and 4 tablespoons for the apples
- pinch of salt

What to do

1. Preheat oven to 180° C/350° F.
2. Sift flour and salt into a large bowl and add butter. Rub together until mixture is crumbly.
3. Mix in sugar.
4. Peel, core, and chop the apples.
5. Place the apples in a pan with a tablespoonful of water and 4 tablespoons of sugar. Cook over a low heat for 5 minutes.
6. Put the apples in an ovenproof dish and cover with the crumble mixture.
7. Place in the oven and bake for 20–30 minutes until golden.

My word!

Where do these food-related English words come from?

cake	*kaka*	(Old Norse – from the Vikings)
lemon	*limon*	(French)
kettle	*cetel*	(Roman)

Music

Many people enjoy pop and rock music festivals during the English summer. Glastonbury, Leeds, and Reading Festivals are the best known and attract top singers and bands. The Proms and the Bath International Music Festival are examples of **classical** music festivals held every year.

Flag-waving is a big part of the Proms!

YOUNG PEOPLE

English pop and rock acts are popular worldwide and have been since the Beatles and Rolling Stones in the 1960s and 70s. In the 1980s, bands such as Duran Duran and Culture Club took the United States by storm. Nowadays bands such as Coldplay are popular in the United States and across Europe.

Literature

England has a long tradition of great authors who have become popular around the world. William Shakespeare is one of the most famous, but Jane Austen, Charles Dickens, the Brontë sisters, Agatha Christie, and many others are also very well-known.

Art

Two of the best-known English artists are J. M. W. Turner and John Constable. Constable's paintings were often of Dedham Vale near his home on the Essex-Suffolk border. The area is known today as "Constable country". Turner was famous for his landscape paintings and had one of his pictures shown in an art gallery when he was only 15! There are many art galleries across the country devoted to both traditional and modern art, including works by artists such as Tracey Emin and Damien Hirst.

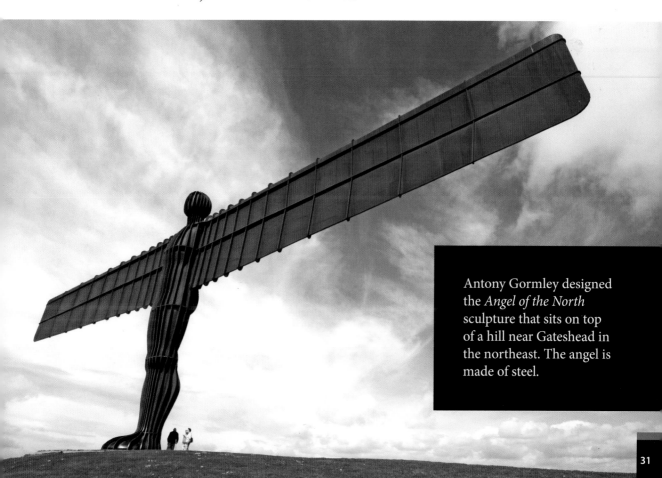

Antony Gormley designed the *Angel of the North* sculpture that sits on top of a hill near Gateshead in the northeast. The angel is made of steel.

Cinema

Going to the cinema is a popular pastime in England for all ages. Many of the films people see are made in the United States but British-made films can often be a big hit, such as *Slumdog Millionaire*. This film helped lead to a rise in the popularity in the West of Bollywood films, made by Indian companies.

Sport

Football is England's most popular sport, both for those watching and playing, but other events attract big crowds, such as Wimbledon and horse racing at Ascot. England usually performs well in water sports such as rowing and sailing. The fact that England is part of an island probably helps as there is plenty of water around!

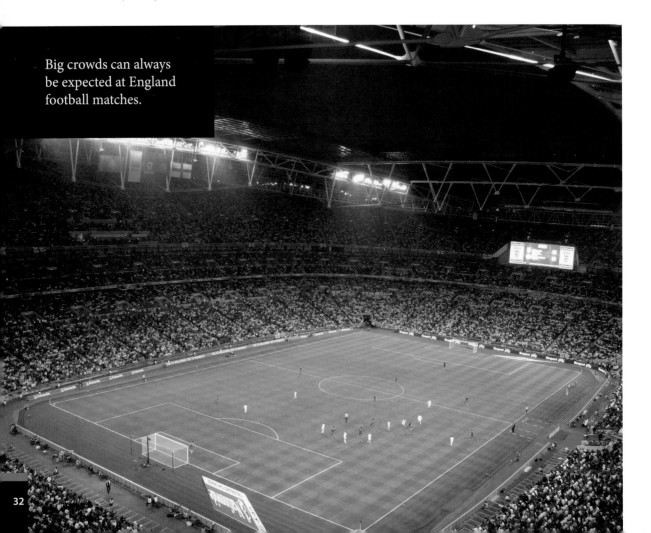

Big crowds can always be expected at England football matches.

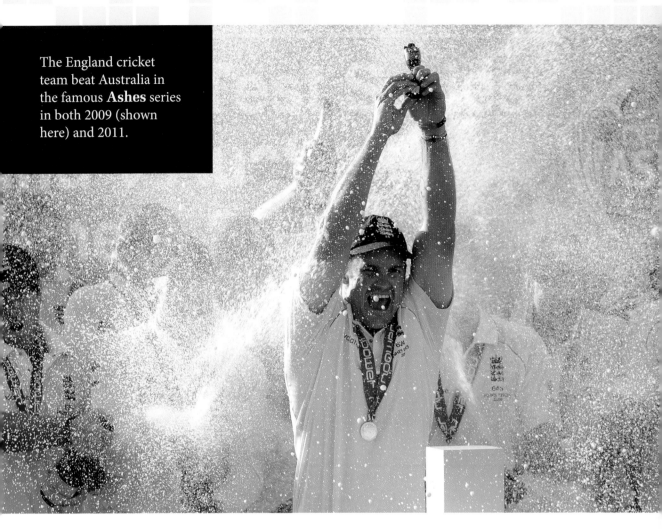

The England cricket team beat Australia in the famous **Ashes** series in both 2009 (shown here) and 2011.

London 2012 Olympics

In 2012 London hosts the Olympics. Improvements have been made in London's transport system. New stadiums and accommodation have been built for the millions of people who will arrive in London to work, take part in, or watch the Olympics.

National anthem

"God Save the Queen", which is actually the British national anthem, is often played at sporting events for the England team. In the **Commonwealth Games** the British nations compete separately so a different song is used. For the 2010 Commonwealth Games the public was asked to vote for this song. They picked "Jerusalem", a song used to **inspire** the England cricket team in the Ashes series in 2005.

Religion

In 2001 about three-quarters of the English population said they were Christian. The next most common religion was Islam, followed by Hinduism. In a more recent poll, about 43 per cent of 16- to 19-year-olds said they do not believe in God.

National holidays

England does not have many national holidays in comparison to other countries. Most are called bank holidays because banks are closed on these days. They include May Bank Holiday and Summer Bank Holiday, and always fall on a Monday. Christmas and Easter are the only religious holidays.

Some other days are celebrated, such as Remembrance Day in November when those who died in wars are remembered. Bonfire Night also takes place in November. People have huge bonfires and fireworks. A straw "guy" is burnt on the bonfire because in 1605 a group of men, including Guy Fawkes, planned to blow up Parliament while the King was there. Fortunately, they didn't succeed!

Festivals and events

Other festivals and events include Notting Hill Carnival in London and maypole dancing, a tradition carried out on May Day, the first day of May. In York there is the Jorvik Viking Festival. The strange but fun cheese-rolling event takes place in Gloucestershire. A cheese is rolled down a steep hill and people chase after it. The winner gets to keep the cheese!

My word!

Most areas of England have their own special words, known as slang:

have a look	*have a mooch*	(city of Birmingham)
money	*splosh*	(city of Liverpool)
house	*hoos*	(city of Newcastle)

These people have dressed up to take part in scenes from history at the Jorvik Viking Festival in York.

England today

England had no strong **national identity** for many years until recently. There is no national dress. At many events where a national anthem is performed, Britain's national anthem is played and no one is even sure what the English anthem is! However, Scotland and Wales gained their own governments in 1999 and this seems to have encouraged more of an English national identity.

Sport is an area that brings the country together and England flags can be seen attached to cars and buildings during events such as the World Cup. England has four-fifths of the UK population and most people live in the southeast of the country. Some of England's cities, such as London and Birmingham, are among the most multicultural places in the world.

Daily life

Many English people love nature and the countryside. Although over 80 per cent live in towns or cities, many people enjoy going to the country for long walks or to see spectacular scenery on their weekends. Parks are popular places for families to visit for a picnic or a stroll.

England: a good place to visit

England has beautiful countryside, interesting weather, and friendly people. Tourists flock to England to see its historical sites and learn about its interesting past. One thing is certain: nowhere in England is far from a castle, national park, country house, or other historical building.

Brighton Pavilion is a royal palace that was built for Prince George (later King George IV) in the late 1700s. He had a wild lifestyle and loved fashionable things.

Fact file

Official language:	English
Capital city:	London
Bordering countries:	Wales and Scotland
Government:	constitutional monarchy
Population:	51,809,700 (in 2009)
Life expectancy at birth (UK):	76.5 years for men; 81.6 years for women; ranked 25th in the world
Religious majority:	Church of England
National symbols:	red rose (flower), oak (tree), three lions (sporting badge)
Area:	130,279 square kilometres (50,301 square miles)
Coastline:	8,982 kilometres (5,581 miles) long
Longest river:	River Thames at 346 kilometres (215 miles) long
Biggest lake:	Lake Windermere at 16 square kilometres (10 square miles)
Highest single-drop waterfall:	Hardraw Force, North Yorkshire
National Parks:	Lake District, Peak District, Northumberland, North York Moors, Yorkshire Dales, Dartmoor, Exmoor, New Forest, South Downs, and the Broads
Lowest point:	Holme Fen at 2.75 metres (9 feet) below sea level
Highest point:	Scafell Pike in the Lake District at 978 metres (3,208 feet)
Currency:	pound sterling
Natural resources:	coal, limestone, clay, gravel
Exports:	chemicals, food, drink
Imports:	food, fuel, machinery

Climate:	temperate
Public holidays:	8 bank holidays
Popularity as a tourist destination:	sixth in the world with 30.7 million visitors per year (2007, UK figures)
Festivals:	WOMAD (music), Glastonbury (music), Bath Festival of Children's Literature, Jorvik Viking Festival
Famous English people:	The Brontë sisters (authors), Agatha Christie (author), David Beckham (footballer), John Lennon (musician), Diana, Princess of Wales, Florence Nightingale (nurse) Charles Darwin (scientist), Margaret Thatcher (prime minister).

My word!

Some people from East London use Cockney rhyming slang when they talk. The slang uses words that rhyme with the word it actually means. Here are a few:

mate	*china plate*
beers	*Britney Spears*
stairs	*apples and pears*
easy	*lemon squeezy*
starving	*Lee Marvin*

England is famous for crafts such as the creation of china and porcelain pots and vases made by Wedgwood. Josiah Wedgwood, grandfather of Charles Darwin, started the company in 1759 and it's still going today.

Timeline

BC is short for "before Christ". BC is added after a date and means that the date occurred before the birth of Jesus Christ, for example, 450 BC.

AD is short for *Anno Domini*, which is Latin for "in the year of our Lord". AD is added before a date and means that the date occurred after the birth of Jesus Christ, for example, AD 720.

700,000 years ago	Evidence shows that people were living in England at this time
around 3000 BC	Stone Age people arrive from Iberian Peninsula
around 3000 BC	Stonehenge is erected
55 BC	Julius Caesar and the Roman army invade England
AD 43	The Roman army successfully invades England, under Emperor Claudius.
around AD 60	Roman army defeats Boudicca, queen of the Iceni
AD 78–80	Romans conquer southern England and Wales, to form a new province called Britannia
AD 410	Romans withdraw from England
AD 449–550	England is separated into different kingdoms ruled by invaders such as the Jutes, Angles, and Saxons
AD 700s	Vikings from Denmark invade England
1066	William, Duke of Normandy wins the Battle of Hastings, and conquers England
1348–1349	Nearly half the population is killed by plague called the Black Death
1362	English is made the official language of Parliament
1534	King Henry VIII becomes head of the Church of England
1536	Act of Union joins England and Wales

1588	The Spanish Armada is defeated by Queen Elizabeth I's navy
1605	Guy Fawkes tries to blow up Parliament
1620	The Pilgrim Fathers sail for America
1707	Act of Union between England and Scotland
1775–1783	American War of Independence takes place, resulting in America becoming a separate country
1700s	Industrial Revolution begins
1918	Women aged over 30 get the vote
1914–1918	World War I
1939–1945	World War II
1979	Margaret Thatcher becomes United Kingdom's first woman prime minister
2005	Terrorist bombings in London
2008	Global financial crisis begins
2010	A General Election leads to the Conservative and Liberal Democrat parties forming a **coalition government**. The Prime Minister is David Cameron.

Glossary

Ashes series of cricket matches, played every two years, between England and Australia

British Empire group of countries that were ruled by Britain in the 19th and early 20th century

broadband type of fast internet connection

Christian related to the religion based on the teachings of Christ

classical serious, artistic music, often played by an orchestra or piano

coalition government temporary alliance between political parties. A coalition government happens when voting has been close and no party has been able to win a majority of the seats in Parliament.

Commonwealth Games games in which Commonwealth nations compete every four years. The Commonwealth includes countries that were part of the British Empire such as New Zealand, Australia, and Canada. The Games involve sports such as athletics, swimming, and boxing.

conservation protection of the environment

culture practices, traditions, and beliefs of a society

currency banknotes and coins accepted in exchange for goods and services

debt money owed to someone else

eco-friendly things that are helpful to the environment, such as recycling

economy to do with money and the industry and jobs in a country

endangered in danger of extinction

European Union (EU) political and economic union of (currently) 27 European countries

export sell goods to another country

Great Plague outbreak of disease in England in 1665. It spread easily from person to person, causing large swellings on the body. As many as 100,000 people may have died.

grocer shop that sells food

habitat environment in which a plant or animal is found

head of state main public representative of a country, such as a queen or president

hedgerow bushes planted in a row and usually used to separate fields

House of Commons first chamber of the law-making body of Parliament. The people choose the 650 Members of Parliament to sit in the House of Commons in a General Election. Each MP represents an area called a constituency.

House of Lords the second chamber of Parliament. Members are not elected but have been chosen by the queen on the recommendation of the prime minister.

import buy goods from another country

Industrial Revolution changes that took place in how goods were made, from small scale production by people to large factories in which machines did most of the work. The Industrial Revolution began in the late 1700s in England.

inspire to affect with a particular feeling such as enthusiasm

landfill site place where rubbish is buried under ground

monarch king or queen who is head of state but has no real power

multicultural mix of people from different cultures and countries

National Curriculum plan of how subjects will be taught in all schools across England

national identity when people feel that they belong to a country and its culture and beliefs

Pope leader of the Roman Catholic Church

ration fixed amount of food that someone is allowed

recession when economic activity slows, unemployment often rises, and interest rates fall, over a period of time

republic country with an elected leader and no monarch

resource means available for a country to develop, such as minerals and energy sources

rural in the countryside

species type of animal, bird, or fish

tax money paid by people to the government. Taxes can come from wages or be placed on goods that people buy.

trade buying and selling of goods, usually between countries

tribe independent social group, historically often made up of primitive or nomadic people

unite bring together

vote to choose. People vote for someone to win an election.

Find out more

Books

Continents in Close-Up: An Illustrated Atlas of Europe, Malcolm Porter
   (Cherrytree Books, 2007)

Countries in Our World: United Kingdom in Our World (Franklin Watts, 2010)

Culture in Action: Twenty-First Century Shakespeare, Elizabeth Raum
   (Heinemann Library, 2010)

Discover Countries: The United Kingdom, Tim Atkinson (Wayland, 2010)

Discover London! Jacqui Bailey (Franklin Watts, 2008)

Exploring Continents: Europe, Jane Bingham (Heinemann Library, 2006)

Famous Lives: Winston Churchill, Katie Daynes (Usborne, 2006)

Great Britons series (Franklin Watts, 2007)

Great Women Leaders: Elizabeth I, Jane Bingham (Heinemann Library, 2008)

Henry VIII and His Six Wives, John Guy (TickTock Books, 2008)

Timelines: The World Wars, Rupert Matthews (Miles Kelly Publishing, 2007)

Websites

www.bbc.co.uk/history/historic_figures
This website has biographies of many of the people mentioned in this
book. You can find out more about Boudicca, William Shakespeare, and
Margaret Thatcher.

www.bbc.co.uk/schools/primaryhistory
Visit this website to learn more about the Anglo-Saxons, children in Victorian
Britain, and children's lives during World War II.

www.eco-schools.org.uk
Learn about the Eco-schools programme on this site.

www.nationalparks.gov.uk/learningabout.htm
Find out more about the UK's National Parks on this government website.

Places to visit

If you ever get the chance to explore England, here are some of the places you could visit:

Arbeia Roman Fort and Museum

This fort on Hadrian's Wall in South Shields shows what life was like in Roman Britain.

British Museum

www.britishmuseum.org

This London museum contains ancient artefacts from Anglo-saxon, Viking, and Roman Britain, as well as other amazing objects from around the world.

East Lancashire Railway

www.east-lancs-rly.co.uk

Have a ride on a steam train!

Jorvik Viking Centre

www.jorvik-viking-centre.co.uk/about-jorvik

Visit this museum in York to learn more about the Vikings and how they invaded England.

Science Museum

www.sciencemuseum.org.uk

Visit the Science Museum in London to find out how science and technology has developed over the centuries.

Stonehenge

www.stonehenge.co.uk

Visit this ancient stone circle in Wiltshire and learn about how and why it may have been built.

Topic tools

You can use these topic tools for your school projects. Trace the map onto a sheet of paper, using the thick black outline to guide you.

The flag of England is called the Saint George's Cross. It is known that the flag has been carried by soldiers in battle from the late 12th centrury, possibly earlier. Copy the flag design and then colour in your picture. Make sure you use the right colours!

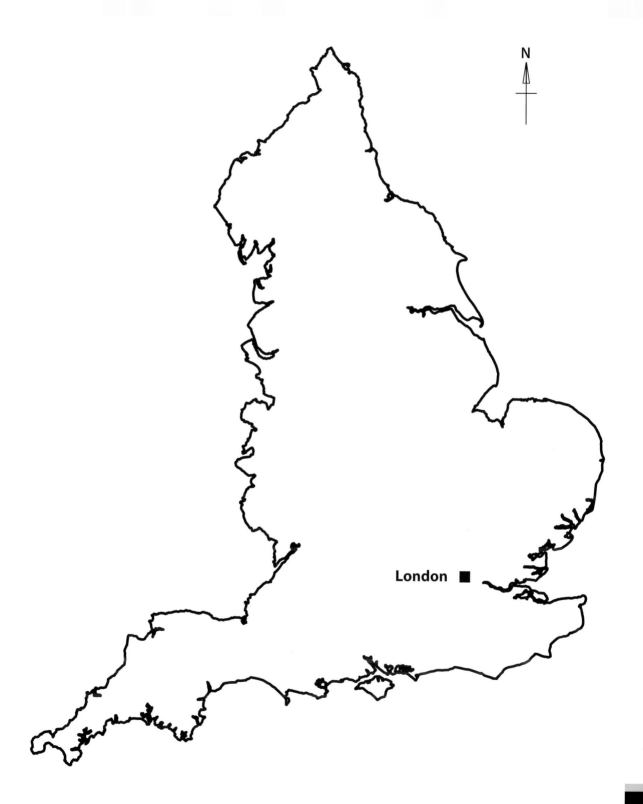

N

London ■

Index

Titles in the series

Afghanistan	978 1 406 22778 9
Brazil	978 1 406 22785 7
Chile	978 1 406 22786 4
Costa Rica	978 1 406 22787 1
Cuba	978 1 406 22788 8
Czech Republic	978 1 406 22792 5
England	978 1 406 22799 4
Estonia	978 1 406 22793 2
France	978 1 406 22800 7
Germany	978 1 406 22801 4
Haiti	978 1 406 22789 5
Hungary	978 1 406 22794 9
India	978 1 406 22779 6
Iran	978 1 406 22780 2
Iraq	978 1 406 22781 9
Italy	978 1 406 22802 1
Latvia	978 1 406 22795 6
Lithuania	978 1 406 22796 3
Mexico	978 1 406 22790 1
Pakistan	978 1 406 22782 6
Poland	978 1 406 22797 0
Scotland	978 1 406 22803 8
Wales	978 1 406 22804 5
Yemen	978 1 406 22783 3